Always With the Questions

ONE POET'S WRITING MANUAL

Also by Marilyn McCabe:

Perpetual Motion
Glass Factory
Rugged Means of Grace
Being Many Seeds

Always With the Questions!

ONE POET'S WRITING MANUAL

Marilyn McCabe

THE WORD WORKS
Celebrating 50 Years

Always With the Questions © 2025 Marilyn McCabe

Reproduction
of any part of this book
in any form or by any means,
electronic or mechanical,
except when quoted in part
for the purpose of review,
must be with permission
in writing from
the publisher.
Inquire of:

THE WORD WORKS
P.O. Box 42164
Washington, D.C. 20015
editor@wordworksbooks.org

No part of this book may be used
or reproduced in any manner
for the purpose of training
artificial intelligence
technologies
or systems.

Author photograph:
Cover design: Susan Pearce Design
Cover Art: Jennifer Sattler

ISBN: 978-1-944585-53-2

*for the WMDs, the Boiler Housers,
my fellow workers in the fields of the word,
and my blog readers, especially those
who took a moment to say,
"Yeah, me too!"*

Contents

PART ONE: The Writing Process

    I.   Please Pass the Butter / 13
    II.   Poem as Impulse and Idea / 15
    III.   Formtion, Functiorm; or, On Navigating Form and Function / 17
    IV.   Very Well Then I Contradict Myself; or, on the First Person Perspective in Poems / 21
    V.   With Sally in the Alley; or, Finding New Ways Into the Poetry Work / 24
    VI.   The Living End; or, On Writing Endings / 26
    VII.   Order! Order!; or, On Finding a Unifying Principle in the Disorderly Poem / 28
    VIII. Shunning the Frumious Bandersnatch; or, Finding the Right Words / 30
    IX.   Mi, a Name I Call Myself; or, More on Voice / 32
    X.   A Real Laugh Riot; or, On Cleverness or Humor in a Poem / 34
    XI.   Time Is on My Side; or, Narrative Motion / 36
    XII.   Who Wrote the Book of Love; or, Remembering Wonder in the Writing Process / 38
    XIII. Working Title; or, Poetry Titles, Oy / 40
    XIV. How Do I Know?; or, Learning to Assess Our Own Work / 42
    XV.   More Better Blues; or, How To Improve / 46
    XVI. Watch Out; or, Creativity and the Power of Standing (Still) / 48

PART TWO: The Revision Process

    I.   Beneath the Skin: Levels of Editing Poems: An Overview / 53
    II.   Do Be Do Be Do; or, the Power and Necessity of Active Verbs / 55
    III.   Line Item; or, On Poetic Lineation / 57
    IV.   On the Sentence / 59
    V.   Word Choice = Tone / 61
    VI.   Syntax; or, I saw a bear driving down the road this morning / 63
    VII.   The Visual / 65
    VIII. And Now to Review / 67
    IX.   The Bigger Picture: Intention / 69
    X.   The Bigger Picture: Doubt / 71
    XI.   Know When to Run; or, When Work in Progress Is Not Making Progress; or, Giving Up as Part of the Poem Editing Process / 73
    XII.   Trust / 75
    XIII. Ambition / 77

PART THREE: Submitting Your Work / 81

PART FOUR: Putting Together a Manuscript:
Everything I Can Think Of

    I.   The Collective / 87
    II.   Ordering the Disorderly / 88
    III.   Filling It In / 90
    IV.   But Wait / 91
    V.   Take a Step Farther Back / 92
    VI.   Where to Begin / 94
    VII. And Then / 95
    VIII. The End / 95

Books and Articles / 97
About the Author / About the Artist / 98
About The Word Works / 98

A Note from the Author:

This book contains excerpts and revisions of blog posts I offered up over the course of ten or so years of thinking about writing poetry. Now I know everything there is to know about it, and no longer need to worry. Just kidding. To understand why and how to write poetry is an ongoing puzzlement and endless source of "Wait, what am I doing?" These are notes from the edge, jottings from the road. I hope you'll find something of use here as I share my own lessons learned (and relearned) (and immediately again forgotten), confusions examined, and strategies attempted. At the end of each section is a little virtual poke in your ribs: a writing prompt in case you thought you would just sit around reading today.

A Note from the Publisher & Instructions:

With delight we offer this, the fourth book in our Word Works Writers' Series. Starting in 2016, we began issuing books that explored and encouraged participation in the poet's quest for meaning, audience, community, and fresh ideas for their work.

In each volume we've tried to provide white space that can be used by the reader to join in the conversation with their own responses along the way. There are extra blank pages in the back of the book, should you run out of space after a prompt that you decide to try.

So far the other books in the series are:

Word for Word: Poems & Prompts (v. 1, *40 Years of Inspiration from The Word Works Poets*), Nancy White, editor.

From the Belly: Poets Respond to Gertrude Stein's Tender Buttons (v. 1, "Objects"), Karren Alenier, ed.

From the Belly: Poets Respond to Gertrude Stein's Tender Buttons (v. 2, "Food"), Karren Alenier, ed.

The glyph above follows most of these mini-essays and precedes a suggested

writing prompt

or suggested reflection to undertake,
as recommended by the author.

# PART ONE:

The Writing Process

I. Please Pass the Butter

Why write poetry? Neruda replies: "It is words that sing, they soar, they descend…Vowels I love… They glitter like colored stones, they leap like silver fish, they are foam, thread, feather, dew…"

Is the impulse to create art inherently an impulse to communicate? Or is it something else entirely?

Poets work in the medium of the word, the medium of "pass the butter," but attempt to enter the realm of that-which-cannot-be-said. I think that's why people get confused about poetry. They expect to encounter the kind of utterance of daily life, or to encounter the basic story structure we've all grown up with, but instead they get this other thing, not entirely visual, not entirely auditory, no butter to pass, nor necessarily a narrative to follow. This attempt to say the unsayable in the medium in which we say the mundane defies logic.

Poems start with a sound, or a phrase, or a word; visual art with a "gesture," as dance. However we start, we creators sense a vacuum and fill it through our medium. Making is a process of following the lead of the original impulse.

In poetry often in the end we edit it out, that thing that got us going. I imagine it's the same in visual art. What is important is how that following goes, how it allows, what leaps we take—and the holding off for as long as possible of intention or meaning-making.

The process of making art is the process of asking questions, of seeking perspective. Even the seemingly simple act of painting a purely representational landscape is an inquiry into the human act of seeing, and into how nature forms and casts color, light, and shadow. Even when I'm not in the act of writing, I'm observing—the furled flag of birch bark flapping wildly in the wind, the sudden snowstorm in the woods coalescing into the stark black and white of woodpecker dashing among trees, and trying to make patterns, sense, to make words from the impulsed utterance of "Oh!"

People read poetry to have the world revealed to them in a new way. Poets mine the power of a good metaphor. A good metaphor is like the twist of the end of a kaleidoscope—briefly the world is fragmented and chaotic, then things fall into place in a new and utterly different way. This is what a good poem does.

*

Write a 1-3 sentence poetry manifesto! "I write because…" Tape it up somewhere and regularly check what you're doing with your writing and how it compares to what you SAID you were doing. Hmm. What's THAT about…?

II. Poem as Impulse and Idea

How do we balance the creative impulse with creative intent? Too much intent can flatten an impulse, like my hair when it gets too long. No body. No bounce. Too much impulse with too little intent is all bounce, all flip-curl.

In the history of talking about learning to write, there has been much attention to "voice"—the finding and nurturing of. I read so many well-voiced things that in the end say little. Other work I read may have interesting thoughts not well said. So it's the two: something to say and a compelling voice to say it with.

But there must be something to be said. And that takes suspending oneself in the sink of the inner self (to shove the trope onward—I really do need a haircut...) and let the water and suds flow down.

I think that deep sense of self from which some authentic art can form might be accessed—and here again is an ongoing theme for me—through play. When I think about play I think about tearing things up and putting them back together again. I think about giving voice to inanimate objects. I think about that edge of giddiness, that burble of laughter in the chest that hasn't quite come out yet.

In Brenda Hillman's article "Cracks in the Oracle Bone" at PoetryFoundation.org, she states, "It is common to hear students talking about 'the idea behind the poem.' There is no idea 'behind' a poem, I say. The words and their phrases are what we have." This troubles me. If there is no idea behind a poem, then what is the poem?

Maybe I'm misunderstanding her use of the word "idea." But idea, after all, is, etymologically, from words meaning to see, and form and pattern. I guess I've just made her point. The poem is the idea, the observed/experienced then captured in form and pattern. Maybe I'm misunderstanding the notion of "behind."

I guess I'm thinking about the impulse, the deep consideration, and the ambition that I think is required to be "behind" a poem. One of the things I struggle with in reading poetry is feeling the originating impulse, and following the poet's ambition for the poem.

I suspect what disturbs me sometimes is that some poems have insufficient impulse, and foreshortened ambition, and too shallow a consideration. (Of course, this is what torments me in my own writing.) But how can I tell who is falling short: me (the reader) or the poet and the poem?

This is my ongoing challenge: to accept the poem as idea, and stop trying to peer "behind" it, but rather explore it as I would explore any idea—questioning (argumentative as I am by nature) and rolling with the ride. (But I've never been one for rollercoasters.)

Only when I plunge into the editing process will I discover what there is in and behind any given draft.

And I think a writer's voice can change, should be allowed to change, maybe ought to change to best meet what the author has to say with any given impulse and intent.

Sometimes I find my most interesting thoughts come when I'm NOT sitting at my desk in front of my notebook. My thoughts can be more free and random when I'm not earnestly awaiting a good thought. Once a week for a month, write in a strange place—at a bus stop, on the toilet, in the dark. When you look back, did changing your locale shift at all what you wrote about?

III. Formtion, Functiorm; or On Navigating Form and Function

I had been working on a multipart essay when I wondered if it was really a sectioned poem. So I spent days and days easing, tapping, tweaking, clipping each segment into lineation, attention to rhythm, structures, and all the various things that poetic forms allow/require of us. And now I'm not sure it works.

But the process has been interesting. On the one hand, the poeming process helped me make the language and sentences more taut and efficient, catch repetitions, reorder thoughts. Creating lines and breaks allowed me to inject additional suggestions into the ideas, or even with a line break subvert what I was saying, or at least question it. But too often, the lines gave gravitas to places I didn't really want emphasized. It made some ideas too weighty, too self-important. Some ideas I wanted to slip in with more subtlety, subtlety that demands of lineation did not seem to allow. So I'm going to take the newly taut language and spread it back out, give some fat back to some of the sentences, allow a more languid pace.

But I also realized that one thing I was looking for in this poetic exercise was another layer of thinking, or a honing of direction. I didn't find that. I read a novel recently and thought, "Hmm, that was a pretty interesting idea in search of a good story to find itself inside. This wasn't it." I fear that's what I have on my hands. I keep thinking function will follow form. If I make it a play, I'll figure out what I'm trying to get at. Maybe an opera. Perhaps it's best as a haiku. Sometimes I can't write my way out of my own way.

Someone asked me recently what kind of constraints I put on my work. I didn't understand the question. Constraints? You mean, other than my own vast limitations? Hunh? But what he meant was the kind of thing poets do sometimes, challenge themselves to write within limits: for some of us free-verse people that might mean writing within a form such as a sonnet or villanelle or the dread sestina; or it make take the form of play: write a poem without using the letter e; or use only a ten-syllable line; or use six random words from the dictionary.

I have had spasms of trying to write in form. I still shudder to remember the crap I've written. Sometimes my poems do, though, begin to take the form of a form: I've had poems that seem to take the shape of a sonnet, have had poems begin to exhibit a rhyme scheme, or that show the kind of obsession a form like a villanelle brings out. I could be more willing and try to be more able at encouraging/allowing that, and making the best of it. But to start out with the intention to write in a form? It makes me shudder.

As for the other tricks, the only thing I do—and this only when I haven't been writing at all—is substitution. That is, I'll take someone else's poem, ideally someone whose work is different from mine, so I'm off-balance to begin with, and then word by word substitute my own words, but as opposites. So "…while I pondered weak and weary" becomes "after we made assumptions, burly and full of ourselves," perhaps. I do this to shake up my work, or push me into process when I've lapsed into lassitude.

They do feel like tricks, these constraint games. And I feel like I can feel the artifice in the final product. Which for some people is the point. My own mind, imagination, abilities, proclivities, ignorances, prejudices, blindnesses, laziness, insistence on some kind of logic…well…etcetera… are constraint enough. Aren't they?

I want the poem to become its own organic thing, growing in bumps and spurts to whatever lumpy, limpy, or suave form it fits itself. My job is to give it some oomph and stay out of the way.

Some would argue, though, that working within constraints requires the imagination rise to a new occasion. Hmph.

And haven't I nudged myself before for the active engagement of the imagination? Hmph.

Maybe it's sonnet that hard. Maybe I shouldn't get my pantoums in a bunch. Maybe terza rima in me yet. Mayb it's tim for somthing nw.

In his book *Draft No. 4: On the Writing Process*, John McPhee shares his approach to writing, all the things he's learned over his long career, primarily as a staff writer for the *New Yorker*. What I have loved about John McPhee is how he manages to be transparent in his telling of his tales. It's like he's standing behind you, just out of range of your peripheral vision, but speaking into your ear, whether he is narrating a raft trip down the Colorado or trying to explain the many geologic folds of the Eastern seaboard.

But he is also generous in offering readers a glimpse into his thought process as he has put together some of his classic stories. The most interesting essay to me, and useful in thinking about poetry, was "Structure." He talks about the process of trying to figure out where to start a story, not to mention where to end it.

And as a poet, I appreciate this dilemma. I often find, both in terms of genuine interest, and in terms of energy, the power of a poem often starts several lines after I think the poem starts. I often find this in other people's poems as well, people who have entrusted me to look at an early draft and comment. Other people have characterized it as "throat clearing."

But McPhee usefully talks about the structure of a story, and how you can potentially start anywhere in the structure. As I don't tend to write narrative, or story-telling, poems, this does not entirely apply to me, but the idea that a poem or a story need not start at what might be considered "the beginning" is useful.

Yes, sometimes you need to set a stage, or lead a reader in to a situation, or give a little back story, but often the most effective thing to do is to start *in media res*, the middle of things. This is why a useful editing exercise is to cut the poem in half and start with the middle section and see what happens. Maybe the top half goes on the bottom, or is best slid in somewhere after the middle, so a back and forth effect is created, or maybe the top half gets tossed, because it's not pulling its weight.

McPhee has often created fairly elaborate diagrams to understand the basic structure of his story, and then decides what event markers can make good starts and ends. In fact, the essay itself rambles around a bit, and crosses back on itself, and occasionally tried my patience, as sometimes his work has done. But I appreciated the journey, as I almost always do.

He emphasizes, though, that the structure of the telling must come out of the story itself. And isn't that true of a poem, too.

Which brings me back to that essay I mentioned earlier that I worked toward a poem structure. (Actually, I almost always start my writing in prose, stretching in to the topic, then I dive into the process of introducing the tools of a poem.) I found when I began that process of turning that essay poemward, I got some visceral reactions. No no no, something said. The line breaks almost made me sick to my stomach to look at. I took them out, let the lines roll out and breathed a sigh of relief. Whatever this thing was, and it might be that puzzling beast we call a "prose poem," it wanted to stretch out, it wanted to wander and linger.

And I also started to jumble what came first, in the end cutting out sections and shuffling them around like a card shark, in much that intuitive process in which I try to put together collections of poems. (Much more on this in section IV. Hang in there.)

Tony Hoagland in a lecture I attended usefully talked about how attention must be paid to how the reader is asked to enter the poem: marched through a wide-open door, slid through a half-open window, or thrown into the deep end of a pool?

McPhee described the process in one story of realizing that an encounter with a bear that happened, in chronological terms, about three-quarters of the way through the narrative, could serve to shape the entire piece. So, understanding that particular story as a circle, he started with the bear, and everything else led back to that moment. It seems like a good idea to start with a bear.

I find often people are committed to the chronological narrative of what they're talking about in a poem, and can get visibly shaken when it's suggested that they throw that chronology out the window. I was thinking about this while reading Diane Seuss's poem "Still Life with Turkey."

The center of the poem is her recollecting being asked, when she was a young child, if she wanted to view her father in his coffin. She said no, and the poem reflects on her role now as someone thirsty for seeing. So the poem starts with sight, not the father but a turkey in a still life: "The turkey's strung up by one pronged foot..." The poem lingers on the turkey for a few lines, then wanders to the memory, reflects then, "...Now I can't get enough of seeing..." and ends with the turkey: "...the glorious wings, archangelic, spread/as if it could take flight, but down,/downward into the earth."

The journey of the poem, like the journey of a story, should start with—and take you to—the bear.

Find a poet who writes poems completely unlike your own. Pick a shortish poem and do the substitute game, relaxing into it and letting your mind pop up words to put in. When you're done, see how it's forced you into new terrain, but then start revising back toward your own voice and style of writing. Can you make it your own? What can you learn from this poet?

IV. Very Well Then I Contradict Myself; or, on the First Person Perspective in Poems

I have worried sometimes about my use of "I" in poems. The "I" is certainly not always me; sometimes it is a character or a handy perspective point for the observations around which it is wrapped, a simple first-person eye-to-the-telescope. The tricky thing with the "I" is that often for an effective poem, the "I" can't be too full of itself. It cannot stand in the way of the reader.

Sometimes the "I" is useful for starting a poem, but then it might need to be edited out as, in the writing, the poem becomes more about what that "I" saw than about the "I" seeing. What is the correct balance for an effective poem between the "I" doing the seeing and the thing seen? If the "I" is needed, there needs to be enough transparency in the "I" that it can easily become you-the-reader.

This makes me think of a larger philosophical question about the self. This is the wonderful writer Olivia Laing from her book *To the River*: "...is it not necessary to dissolve the self if one hopes to see the world unguarded?"

It occurs to me that to make good art, there does need to be a dissolution of the "I" but then possibly its re-creation as a vehicle for the art, an eye for the seeing.

Which makes me think about a rhetorical question posed in an introduction to a poet at a reading I went to recently, a question I thought was supremely dumb. The introducer asked: "Are all poems self-portraits?" Of course they are/are not and what's your point? Of course they are a product of wild imagination shaped by the individual experiences of the writer, and a fake wig and glasses, or stripped down to nude and dancing a watusi. I mean, really. Then there are issues of form, function, experimentation, imitation.

Which loops me back to the "I" and who the "I" is or who it can be. Bertrand Russell wrote: "An individual human existence should be like a river—small at first, narrowly contained within its banks, and rushing passionately past rocks and over waterfalls. Gradually the river grows wider, the banks recede, the waters flow more quietly, and in the end, without any visible break, they become merged in the sea, and painlessly lose their individual being."

I think that merging occurs, in a poem, through the use of visceral verbs and vivid images, not through words that represent emotions. No "I felt" but the depiction of a body feeling, a body in the world.

I am rererereading the excellent book by Vivian Gornick on writing, *The Situation and the Story: The Art of Personal Narrative*. Although the book is about writing personal essays and memoir, she says so many smart things that are absolutely applicable to writing poetry.

She talks about being "engaged at the deepest level" where "writing does not wander about on the page accumulating description for its own sake, or developing images independent of thought, or musing lyrically. The point of view originates in the nervous system and concentrates itself in the person of a narrator who...is to use the narrating self only to shape those associations that will provide drive and lead on to inner resolution."

This presence of the narrating self to the situation creates the "story," or, I argue, the effective poem. I'm not talking just about the confessional poem. I'm talking about any poem in which the poet engages with the world and is spurred to write out of that engagement.

Poems that lack it might be interesting, but I guarantee you won't carry them folded up in your wallet for times of trouble, or quote them at relevant life points, or carry a book of them with you through eleven apartment moves. Gornick talks about finding the other in the self and using that self-investigation to provide purpose and tension in an essay or memoir. But isn't that also the case in poetry—is there not a crucial element of investigation, and aren't we often asking questions of our selves? And must they not be so intimate that you, the reader, are also engaged in that self-same self-investigation, advertently or inadvertently? We are each, as Gornick puts it, "a mind puzzling its way out of its own shadows."

About this idea of "truth" in a piece, Gornick writes: "What happened to the writer is not what matters; what matters is the large sense that the writer is able to make of what happened." It seems to me this is as true in poetry as in any kind of literature.

Of course, this is not what all poets are about. Some are functioning on the surface of sound, or the whiteness of page and what can be played out there, or are at some other kind of poetic enterprise. Maybe my thinking here is too narrow. I am writing about the kind of poetry she talks about: "looking for the inner context that makes a piece of writing larger than its immediate circumstance..." That's the kind of poem I'm talking about.

*

Pull at random 5 of your poems that use the first person. Change them all to second person. Change them all to third person, and have a clear sense of who that third person is— someone you know or someone you can clearly imagine or someone randomly you see on the street. Do any of the poems gain anything in the rewrites, or have you gained any fresh perspective on the poems from this exercise of stepping away from the "I"?

V. With Sally in the Alley; or, Finding New Ways Into the Poetry Work

A friend of a friend was told this about writing: It's okay to write about the same damn thing over and over again, but make sure to do it in different ways. Find a new way to approach it each time.

I think of this often. In other words, it's fine that I'm obsessed by a subject matter, with trying to get to some new way of understanding it, but my poems need to approach it by different means. Makes total sense.

But sometimes I catch myself trodding a too-worn path. I *think* I'm trying different things, but all I'm doing really is skirting a bit the old route only to find my way back there again.

One solution I often try in order to shake up my step is to look at art. I like rattling around in the art world looking for something that stops me and twirls me around. Sometimes this dizziment can open a pathway to a new way to approach my own work.

A couple of years ago, as a big, grown-up, middle-aged lady, I decided to take up ballet. It was…well…an experience. I stuck with it for almost a year. I never learned to pirouette, but I did…well…learn to do some toe-pointy things. Anyway. I'm glad I had the idea to disrupt my brain and brain-body connection with this class. It makes me experience the world a little differently, to pay attention differently, and to ask different things of my mind and its connection to my body.

And I think about this as I peruse Lynda Barry's book *Syllabus: Notes from an Accidental Professor*, which is a crazy quilt notebook of the kinds of assignments she gives to her various classes on thinking and paying attention. She uses many kinds of timed assignments for drawing, writing, making notes, listening to passing conversations, telling stories—all in pursuit of maintaining an attentive yet dreaming mind, of being conscious and being conscious of being conscious, without being self-conscious. Many would-be students say to her anxiously, "But I don't know how to draw." But it's in between the not-knowing and doing-anyway that magic happens.

One note from a page of her notebook says this: "How the brain works when we refrain from concentration, rumination, and intentional thinking—"

It's when my mind is alert but a bit flighty, like I'm humming and skating at the same time—I can't be too distracted from the skating, or I'll hit a bump in the ice and fall down; and I can't be too focused on humming, because, well, that would be kind of crazy—that I come up with some good ideas, and can start to bring them to fruition.

In the region of Sussex, England, there's a specific word for the little gap at the base of a hedgerow, a passageway made from the regular coming and going of a small animal: a smeuse.

Looking at art, listening to music, watching dance—this can reveal to me the smeuses of others' passages, one I might ease through myself. And in so doing find a new way to run at the same old topic.

Take yourself to someplace that has some art: a museum, a gallery, a coffeeshop with some local artist's work on the walls, or pick an art book at random from the library. Find a work that really speaks to you. Give yourself over to it and then set a timer for ten minutes and write whatever comes to you. Then find a work that does not interest you at all. Spend some time really looking at it and then do the same ten minute write. Don't stop writing in those ten minutes. Push past those moments when you may feel you have nothing to say. Write that. Then keep writing.

VI. The Living End; or, On Writing Endings

I'm good at beginnings. I can begin a million things. I just often can't figure out how to end them. I think I have been writing poetry because of my anxiety about endings—by virtue of the relatively short nature of poems, my how-will-I-end-it anxiety is shorter too. This is why I've found writing essays and fiction so grueling and unpleasant. But even writing poems I find myself reaching with increasing desperation for an ending, sometimes long before I've even figured out what I'm writing about.

At least I'm aware of it—admitting you have a problem is the first step, right? So I start to recognize my end-times anxiety and purposely both relax and try to continue writing through it, trying this direction and that, trying to get myself to write right onward, toward any number of endings, writing even past an ending, so I can make sure I've said what the poem wants to say.

I got a critique once about a group of poems that they all fell toward their endings with a similar move, so I have to watch my tendency to wrap things up in the same way, to be too tidy. Another poet told me I had a tendency to write poems that were closed-ended rather than open-ended, so I need to think about this often. Geesh, it's no wonder I have anxiety.

Another commented on a number of my endings, and offered several alternatives, none of which I liked. Yet another offered a new ending to a poem, which I took, then published with that ending. But now when I read the poem aloud in readings, I always revert to my original ending.

My mother is very old and I fear her ending—at the moment she's at least overtly physically healthy, if absent her memory, but I fear her end will be slow and painful, as so many old people's ends can be. How can I balance my concern for her ending with my concern for her continued life? I have similar fears for my poems as I write them. I want them to die well. Well, no, I want them to live well, and to end well. What's that sentiment about sliding up to the pearly gates yelling "woo woo"? I want that for my poem endings.

Too often I've had the experience of a piece of writing never "in the end" revealing to me what it was really trying to figure out, so I loop around and around until I give up, or shove some ending on it like a cork. When I'm very lucky, a poem falls gracefully to some image that says it all. Or, and again, this takes luck, I find the ending right there at the beginning, and realize I've just written the whole poem upside-down.

As a child I loved to hang upside-down on the handrail of our walkway, or off the couch watching TV upside-down. Lately I've been missing that perspective on things, and no amount of downface-dog or head-standing quite replicates the bliss of just hanging around in reverse of the known world. So if you come to my door and think you see feet instead of a head sticking up above the couch, well, I'm busy.

*

Pick 5 of your poems at random. Rewrite them all from the bottom up. Rewrite them all starting halfway down, flipping the beginning to the end. Did you discover anything interesting in the process? Did any of those rewrites zing?

VII. Order! Order!; or, On Finding a Unifying Principle in the Disorderly Poem

I have been trying a new approach to writing poems these days, very different for me, who usually has a stranglehold on word and idea. I've been kitchen-sink-ing it these days. I start with an image, and anything that occurs to me around that image which seems at all relevant to why the image caught my eye, I throw down on paper. And I do this for a while, leaving a file open on my desktop to add stuff to as it occurs to me as I wander around my day. After a while I start rereading them to rediscover what's there. If it seems like I've got a heap of stuff that has some relation—a bunch of silverware perhaps, or cups and saucers—then I pick through to try to create short, more orderly passages. I try to find threads to weave and gaps to fill. I toss to the bottom things that either don't seem to quite fit or are blathery or boring, but I don't want to throw away just yet.

Often I find similar versions of the same idea, so I have to decide which one is most interesting, or twist a handle here, ding a tine there, so there's enough different that I can keep them both. And I start to try line breaks, stanza thingies, start to clip and shift my way toward rhythms. And I try to find the point beyond which an idea I've thrown in just cannot stay.

It's in this thinking process that I bring some order to the mess. I do insist, it seems, on having some kind of organizing principle or through-line of reason. It's more satisfying for me both as a writer and a reader to make sure there's some kind of connective tissue at work in a poem, a line of thinking that at least somewhat clearly loops back upon itself.

I want the reader to happily take leaps with me, not find themselves legs flailing over an abyss. It doesn't always work, of course. I have heard from some of my readers of their Wile E. Coyote-like positions all dingetdingetydingety over a poetic cliff. They don't care for it, I hear.

Some of these poems I'm working seem to want to stay long and unwieldy; some hope to strike out across the page width-wise as well as length-wise; one floundered itself into an essay form instead of poem; one just got whittled down from four pages to one stanza. I'm not sure if any of them quite add up yet to more than the sum of their parts. But I'm enjoying the process at the moment. This devil-may-care flinging of stuff into the sink with a clatter.

But I guess the question remains: *How* do I go about finding or high-lighting the thread among the disparate pieces of a poem? It has something to do with theme, and something to do with imagery. For example, I'm working on a piece that uses repeated imagery of a bridge to talk about, well, various bridgey ideas, both literal and figurative. Movement, transition, change, stasis, choice-making, connection, communication: all things I'm thinking around as I think about this bridge.

One thing I threw in was a segment not about the bridge I was standing on, but the bridge in my mouth, and tied it back in to the road sort of bridge, and to an idea about trust and connection sort of. I think I may be able to let that stay. I think I manage to have enough of a string that it stays attached to the whole. Another section talks about alignments of standing stones in France that may act as a bridge for the gods, or for human beings to move between life and death. That section strikes me as going too far off the image and the collection of ideas, so I think I'm going to jettison that one. Neither the image nor the idea are quite enough in keeping with everything else going on in the…well…whatever this thing is, poemy thing or essayish thing.

So the answer to *how* seems to be a constant querying of each thing I throw in to the kitchen sink and a check back to look at the whole confabulation. What have I thrown in, and will it find its way to fit with the whole group? If I'm setting a table with silverware, I may not need a cowbell.

*

Choose a few of your troublesome poems. Cut them into segments a line or two each. For each, randomly choose segments and lay them out in the order you chose them. What reveals itself as you read this new arrangement, what surprises?

VIII. Shunning the Frumious Bandersnatch; or, Finding the Right Words

I was listening to something the other day when it occurred to me that the writer had used all these multisyllabic words that were buzzing around my face like annoying flies, getting in the way of the words that were actually saying something. (I was reminded of a regular commentator on my local public radio station who would lugubriously and with ponderous solemnity pontificate his cogitations and deliberations with as many multisyllabic appellations as he could prestidigitate. I would turn the radio off when he came on and snort several good monosyllabic Anglo-Saxon words at it.)

Suddenly, inside all those words flailing around, I heard a phrase of five short words that all by themselves made a satisfying gong that shattered the buzzing of those long words, that resonated with meanings and suggestions and layers.

This is what writing and its vital partner, revision, are all about: shuffling through the noises to find the satisfying and resounding gong.

In the structure of a poem, each word, as an I-beam or a column, needs to be carrying weight and be balanced with the others, or deliberately off-balance. Multisyllabic words have to be used carefully because they can visually and sonically outweigh other words. They also run the risk of sounding self-conscious. (Why use "utilize" when "use" will do, except that you think it sounds fancier?) (Or maybe you need three beats in that line, I suppose. That might be a justification...but a pretty shaky one.)

Similarly, grand and abstract words can weigh too much: love, for example, soul, universe. Even "moon" has to be handled with care. (I was advised once to not use the moon at all, as it's been sooooo overdone. But, I mean, geez, I can't NOT talk about the moon.)

It takes patience, and humility, I think, to not get caught up in my own extensive vocabulary options, to instead wait for, or dig for the often more simple utterance that says more than its parts. And then to have the courage to surround it with silence, the vital partner of speech.

*

You're amassing a collection of poems. I know you are. Go through every one of them and cast a hairy eyeball at the multisyllabic words. Are they earning their keep? Or can a simpler word cast a better spell?

IX. Mi, a Name I Call Myself; or, More on Voice

My friend and fellow poet David Graham recently wrote to me, "I've finally come to believe that 'voice' is not something to concern myself with. Others will or will not tag me with such a thing, but it just messes me up to think about it. I simply (ha! it ain't simple!) try to write as well as I can & in the process figure out what I want to say (which for me always happens in the revision process, not before.)...In a similar way, worrying about originality is for me mostly a dead end. I love something Levertov said: 'Originality is nothing else but the deepest honesty.'"

I thought about that for a while, and replied, "I wonder if it's not the author that has a voice but the poems themselves. I know I get annoyed when a poem of mine starts having a kind of woff woff self-aggrandizing tone of some British lord or Oxford don. I have to shove it off its high horse. Then other poems just think they're so damn funny they start laughing at themselves so hard I can't understand what they're saying."

And soon after that exchange I found this notion by Richard Russo in the eponymous essay of his new book *The Destiny Thief*: "I'd been told before that writers had to have two identities, their real-life one...as well as another, who they become when they sit down to write. This second identity, I now saw, was fluid, as changeable as the weather, as unfixed as our emotions. As readers, we naturally expect novels to introduce us to a new cast of characters and dramatic events, but could it also be that the writer has to reinvent himself for the purpose of telling each new story?"

That feels both interesting and true. I don't think it's contradictory to think about an author's voice and the voice of a poem or a story. Both voices exist, creating a mini chorus with every piece.

As I look back on my work, I discern a certain McCabeness about most of it, even as the tone and timbre, rhythm and diction, snap or murmur, are quite different. (Although I confess, I sort of feel like if I've read one Russo book, I've read them all....)

How else to explain this than there is a voice in the poem itself that it's my job to summon in creating it and honing in revision? And yet because of the limitations of my own self (even with all its multitudes) the range of voices summoned in the poems will be limited as well, and will sound like me without my trying, or worrying too much about it. If my poems sound too much like someone else, then, as David indicates, I'm probably not clear on what I'm trying to say and am not working from that "deepest honesty," and it's my job in the revision process to sort that out.

So this idea of "finding your voice" may be like so many other classic pieces of advice—overly simplistic, often taken too far, yet containing some useful truth. Like "write what you know" or "never lend money to friends." Well, yes...but, I have this thing called an imagination. And I could really use $20. I guess you find your voice by finding your deepest concerns and writing from some authentic core. Or that's the task, anyway. Easier said than...well...said.

*

What, when you think about it too hard, scares the crap out of you? What fear inside you can you only look at sideways with your eyes slitted up? Breathe into that fear and then write for ten minutes without stopping. Catch your breath. Then do it again. Try not to name the fear. Use images to define it.

X. A Real Laugh Riot; or, On Cleverness or Humor in a Poem

In response to a conversation about "voice," a recent critiquer of a poem of mine averred that in two particular places I had "substituted cleverness for humor." This gave me paws. Ha ha, see what I did there?

Isn't cleverness humor? Humorous? Humor-ish? Is it a lesser form of humor?

It could be said to be superficial, perhaps—wordplay, for example, whereas humor, perhaps, should dig deep, have a little of its tragedian partner. Is there not room for cleverness in a poem?

The first place the critiquer red-penned in this way was indeed wordplay. I was trying to reconsider the meanings of a word. But maybe I had made my point with the image I presented, and didn't need to emphasize it with the wordplay. In which case, it wasn't the cleverness at fault but the redundancy. Fair enough.

The second offense was a quick lightening of the mood—I used an old song lyric to describe a situation. I'm not quite so convinced cleverness was a problem there (or indeed, anywhere). In the poem in question there are a few lighter moments in a poem otherwise taking itself seriously, and this was one of them. Can't a little levity allow the reader to take a breath, to share with the writer a chuckle?

But maybe such cleverness calls too much attention to the writer. Look at me and my cleverness, it may say, and take the reader out of the poem in a way that is harmful to the poem and its atmosphere. Do we really need to share a wink, you and I?

If I want to inject humor, shouldn't it be of the deeper kind and arise from the poem itself, not from the author's ego? I don't know. I like to laugh. But when is humor organic to a poem and when is it hiding something or asserting itself in a show-offy way? I just don't know. But I think it's an interesting question.

*

> *Write a poem that begins with a joke line, such as,* Why did the chicken cross the road?, *or* A priest, a rabbi, and an imam walk into a bar, *or* Knock knock... ***But proceed toward something very serious. Can you conjure the comedy/tragedy balance?***

XI. Time Is on My Side; or, Narrative Motion

I am thinking about time, that mover, that crawler, how it shuffles, how it disappears. I began thinking about this as I have been doing an online course on the braided essay, that is, a prose beast that contains two or more through-lines of thought/experience, the weaving of which can create a conversation, as one line questions, highlights, casts shadows on the others, or creates gaps of warp and weft such that new ideas are suggested.

I had read an example of such a thing, but found myself speed-reading in boredom through it. And I posited that I was bored because none of the threads contained a narrative that moved through time. I wondered if I needed that pull of story to carry me forward, that sense of time passing and something unfolding. I don't know if that is actually the case, because I can't be bothered to go back and reread it to test my theory.

But in poetry my preference to read and to write is for the lyric poem, the poem-of-a-moment, of held breath, a blink-and-now-it's-gone. So why this testiness when it came to prose? To be fair, maybe it was just that one essay. I'm reading various works by my latest literary crush Robert MacFarlane. His works are not set in moving time, particularly, yet I find them fascinating. The narratives are of short duration—a hike here, a conversation there. Maybe there are just enough of those to keep me turning the page, maybe it's that, not the magic of his lyrical prose.

The movement of time on the page is prestidigitation: one moment you're in the dining room, the next, five years have passed and you're on a train. The tick tick of life lived is never that gratifyingly flee-full of the ache of passing time: boredom, the dentist's waiting room, the wait for the other shoe to drop. Yes, there is the sending the child off to kindergarten one day and college seemingly the next, the panic that time has passed that you haven't noticed.

But is that not also ache?

But maybe it's not the passage of time that helps pull the reader along, but in fact, some indication of change—whether in the narrator, in the situation, in the unfolding comprehension of what is occurring. Long ago I attended a creative nonfiction writing workshop, and it was suggested that my essay about my decision to quit my job was too blame-y of everyone else. I was taken aback by this perspective, as I didn't think that that was what I was doing. But I think back now and suspect that what I had not sufficiently done was to express the internal change that had lead me to that point—had not shown the eagerness turned dread, the hope turned to despair.

Time is change, and change occurs in time. So whether the expression in writing is "later that day" or "I had thought once X but finally realized Y," the readerly imagination is caught and carried. But of course that inner change is the more satisfying thread to follow, the emotional trip always more deeply interesting than the movement of the minute hand or the walk from point A to point B. But it's the harder story to tell.

*

Write a lyric poem about ten years of your life. Write a narrative poem about a moment.

XII. Who Wrote the Book of Love; or, Remembering Wonder in the Writing Process

The other night I was listening to a writer read a long descriptive piece. The scene obviously meant a lot to the writer/reader, but failed to reach me. It's not that I couldn't picture what was being described—the description was perfectly picturable, and I could understand what would move the person to write it in a diary. But to make a work of art of it, to make a "poem," something else needed to happen.

What is the problem, here? I speculated. What can I learn? As I listened, it occurred to me: a.) the language needed to capture viscerally the moment—verbs needed to be active, adjectives vivid; b.) the imagery needed to be imaginitive enough to capture the emotion, and to give dimension, layers, senses; and c.) nothing was unknown to the writer/reader. What could have been meditative and transcendent instead was not, for me.

Where, I wondered to myself, was the actual wonder? What was discovered by the writer in writing this? What in this accounting surprised the writer or moved the writer or forced the writer to think harder, to be momentarily confused, startled, to shiver, to shake a head or a fist, to question perception, sanity, to feel dizzy with something?

There was an allusion to time: ephemerality and timelessness, but it was almost tossed in there half-heartedly, even though, I think that's exactly what was at the heart of the thing. And finding the heart of the thing is the whole enterprise, isn't it?

And by heart I don't mean that easily achieved shape with two bumps at one end and a point at the other, but the whole mysteriously pumping, sucking and spewing, occasionally off-beated blump or hoosh, or, awful silence, the blupping and forceful chug of this vital organ.

I wanted to shake the reader and say, "Okay, you've told us what you know; now show us what you've got."

What we want to be doing is writing through the known into the not-known. I always forget this until I remember again. And so I say that to myself today, as I face the abyss of page, as I think, how do I say this unsayable thing. I wonder.

Wonder, it turns out, is a mystery word; its origins unclear, but many Germanic languages have a version of it—wundor, wundrian, wunder. So that got me thinking about some synonyms. Amaze is from the OE *amasian* meaning stupefy or stun but may have had an original sense of being knocked on the head unconscious (those Old Norse roustabouts). This word actually led to the word maze, rather than the other way around, but which started as a word describing a state of mind—dazed, delusional—and then became a structure to effect that end.

Astonish, astound, and that ilk came from *extondre*, meaning leave someone thunderstruck, from the Latin verb to thunder, *tonare*, which, traced back, apparently just means noise. And I think of those days when the sky is dark and low, foreboding of precipitation, and suddenly you hear, beneath the chatter of the day, that noise, thunder. So as I write I must be listening for the noise under the noise, the thunder of what's coming or what's happening behind those clouds of words on the page. And when I hear thunder, then I wait. Lightning could be next.

※

Set a timer for ten minutes and write without stopping to finish the phrase "I don't know why...." Then set a timer for ten minutes and write without stopping to finish the phrase "Now I know why...."

XIII. Working Title; or, Poetry Titles, Oy

I'm not saying it was necessarily because of the title changes, but I had the experience once of radically changing titles of two poems that had been rejected several times from lit mags and suddenly and immediately got an acceptance for them. Coinkydink? Possibly. But it certainly made me sit up and take notice of what titles can do.

☞ A title can situate a poem in place or time, so you don't have to use up vital poem real estate with that information. Yeats sets us right on "The Lake Isle of Innisfree," so we're already in place when he begins. But you may run the risk with that of overemphasizing time or place when the point of the poem is to transcend time or place. You have to ask whether the time/place title helps or distracts or gives too much attention to itself.

☞ A title can emphasize a certain *je ne sais quoi* that the poem is getting at. But you run the risk of beating the reader over the head. A title that basically says "Be Prepared to Feel Sad Ahead," or "This Poem Is About Grief" just aren't that interesting. But you can suggest it slantwise with an image, perhaps, or an echo of sound or word/words from the poem. I mean, sometimes it's the only good solution to name a poem about daffodils "The Daffodils." But maybe it's a lost opportunity.

☞ A title can carry some of the weight of the poem, in that you can ask it to act as another line, the first line, in fact. You can ask the title to address the same things that the poem addresses, or hint at them, or choose a title that creates a resonance. A long and searing poem of several parts tracing a personal and family history Ocean Vuong titled "On Earth We're Briefly Gorgeous." There is nothing about earth nor beauty particularly in the poem, but the title captures a tenderness toward the fallible humans considered in it. It prepares our heart somewhat for what lies ahead, and when the poem is done helps settle a kind of grace on the experience.

☞ Or you can choose something completely innocuous, I suppose, and not ask much from a title at all. Modern visual artists do that all the time—"Painting #7 of a Series of 10," for example. But visual artists don't have to work in the medium of words; poets do. (What if visual artists "entitled" their work with splashes of paint or visual gestures instead of words? I think that would be helpful sometimes.)

But we poets work in a world of words and white space, and the title has a particular status at the top of the page. It sits lordly over the poem text, wearing its white robes. It offers an opportunity to capture something about what lies ahead or provide a way to loop from the end back into the beginning again. It can provide crucial information for the reader to find their way into the poem, or set a tone, or cast a lifeline for the reader to hold as they walk through the poem, then out and back in again, or out and out and out into the world.

*

Pick some poems you're struggling with and try making the last line the title, and then come up with a different last line. Does it open up anything?

Pick some poems with innocuous titles and try filching some lines from the poem to use as a title instead.

Take a look at someone else's book of poems. See if you can find poems that could have used a new title, and see if you can come up with one. Take that newfound confidence and turn back to your own poems...

XIV. How Do I Know?; or, Learning to Assess Our Own Work

I encounter again the ubiquitous "Send us your best work" bullshit advisement on the submission page of a literary magazine. Listen. I have never looked at a poem and thought, "Okay, well, this is mediocre, I think I'll send it to x literary magazine." Have never read through a manuscript and thought, "Oh, well, this is better than some of the crap out there, I think I'll send it to x publisher."

You bastards, I *am* sending you what I think, at that moment, is my best work....I think...

Do I read it a week after I've sent it out and think, "Holy crap, what was I thinking?" Sometimes.

Do I get your rejection back and think, "But this is the best work I've ever done and you *still* won't take it?" Sometimes.

Do I get your rejection back and think, "Hmm, well, I think you were right about that"? Sometimes.

The big question is how do we know when our work is at its best. How do we develop within ourselves an adept critical eye. No, really, that's a question. Please tell me: How do I develop within myself an adept critical eye?

Time is a wonderful filter.

If only I would listen to myself and not get overexcited by a new piece and start sending it out in the first blush of blind optimism.

I think I will create a new folder called Hold It! (I'm a great creator of folders...) and put in it every new poem I'm excited about, and I'm not allowed to look at them until at least a month after I've put it in the folder. AT LEAST a month. Six months is probably better.

In six months I'm a different person than six months before—new skin, blood, colon, fingernails, as cells replace themselves throughout the body at varying rates. So surely the new me will have some fresh insight.

I'll have the same eyeballs, though, and mostly the same brain, but new neuronal networks. So in order to shove myself along developmentally, as the pink-faced new poems cool their heels in the Hold It! folder, I should work on my eyesight and my memories. Which means to me that I should read more and widely in poetry especially, and when I find a poem that makes me say "wow, that is good work," spend some time taking a look at how it works at working.

But also other kinds of written work, because all kinds of literature can feed perspective. And I should also look at art, listen to music. And probably dance a little, even if just in my kitchen. These kinds of inputs open the brain to new ways of seeing, ways of communicating, ways to imagine. So when I open that folder again, I can see with altered vision and new light.

Once I do look at the poem again, I should also question myself harder.
- What do I mean here? This is all very fine sounding, but is it more than sound and fancy?
- Have I dug deep enough into the initiating impulse behind this poem? Do I even remember what I thought I was writing toward?
- If I've forgotten, what, then, presents itself to me in this poem, and is it interesting?
- Does energy spark and fade throughout the poem?
- Inquire of that movement: why does it shift, how can I make the whole thing spark and arc?
- Inquire of every stinking word: Does it belong, does it add, does it move, does it shimmer, does it hold water?

Ugh, with such big questions, I fear I may never open up the Hold It! folder again. Wasn't it easier just to love the poem and ship it out and take the rejections as they came?

Reading a poem aloud to myself can be a powerful tool to detect awkwardness, tongue-tangling sounds, tonal oddness. Taking it to an open mic is also a way get even further remove as you cast it into the silence of the room and hear what floats and what falls with a kersplunk. Painful, sometimes, possibly embarrassing, but useful.

I find that the main element required to get some decent perspective is time. I love love love many of my new poems. Then I hate hate hate them. Only with sufficient time can I come to some middle ground of a cooler, less passionate perspective.

Also I have found that putting together collections is a really useful exercise for feeling out weaker poems. My cilia may vibrate a bit, or a lot, when I'm reading through a collection of my own poems, and I've learned to trust this indication that something's not right.

Sometimes the whole poem just has to be removed, sometimes it's a line, and every once in a while, it's not the poem but where it stands in relation to other poems. Sometimes just moving its location can make the cilia calm down.

But how do I know I can trust myself? Northrop Frye wrote, in "The Archetypes of Literature" (*Kenyon Review*), "The fact that revision is possible, that the poet makes changes not because he likes them better but because they are better, means that poems, like poets, are born and not made. The poet's task is to deliver the poem in as uninjured a state as possible, and if the poem is alive, it is equally anxious to be rid of him, and screams to be cut loose from his private memories and associations, his desire for self-expression, and all the other navel-strings and feeding tubes of his ego." This readjusts my perspective—maybe I need to not so much trust myself, but trust the poem. When it's able to walk, it'll walk away. Or run.

You know that collection of poems I know you know you have? Sit down in a space other than where you usually write—go to the library, a coffee shop, a park bench—and read through them all. If something in your body tics or pulls back or winces at certain poems, if your nose wrinkles, an eyebrow raises, your brow furrows, your foot twitches, you sigh, you yawn, pull those poems. The body knows.

XV. More Better Blues

I asked a group what they do to move their poetry to the next level. I got a lot of advice about writing prompts at first. But is the key to writing better poetry writing more? I guess it's a multi-lock door requiring several keys. More is surely not necessarily better. You could just be generating more of the same.

Engaging in translation projects has sometimes, I believe, helped me re-engage with my own work with new spirit, which can lead to work that feels more interesting.

"Read widely in other arenas" is another useful piece of advice, I find. Reading in the sciences often jumpstarts me to try interesting things, which can often make for better work.

Other good advice I've received is to examine my poems' ambitions and in what ways the poems may fall short.

Also, are there things I tend to do in my poems that end up being a crutch or a habit rather than a conscious decision that enhances the poem?

Someone suggested reading outside my comfort zone, which seems like an interesting idea. Although given my tendency to be an impatient and crabby reader, that may not be the route for me.

Another key must be to read more and to read with more of a "how'd this poet pull that off?" eye.

I think the old arts tradition of imitation is a good idea too—painters recreate old master paintings, musicians copy great phrasing, we can write imitations by substituting our own words and leaps and silences into the structure of others' great poems to try to get an intimate sense of how they did what they did.

So anyway, write more, yes, but write more better.

*

Remember that manifesto you wrote? If some time has passed, revisit it. What do you think now? Is it sufficiently ambitious? Is it far-sighted and grand enough for a manifesto? How is what you're writing now measuring up to your grand intentions? Write a new manifesto. Be big. Be bold. Wave your arms around. Tape it up on your wall.

XVI. Watch Out: or, Creativity and the Power of Standing (Still)

My sister, a mental health therapist, has mentioned an approach she uses with some of her clients that she refers to as "posture and purpose," reminding them to keep standing tall both in body and in mind, and to think and continue to move forward. She advises them to raise their eyes often, that this lifting up of the eyes and the face to the sky invokes some of the muscles that also are triggered by a smile.

This reminds me of "dog whisperer" Cesar Millan's advice to maintain a sense of calm assertiveness, and his own upright posture, shoulders back, chest expanded. It also reminds me of voice lessons in which I was asked to feel like a line connected my upper chest to the sky, so I always had an uplifted feeling, allowing capacity of breath, and to keep my eyes looking forward to help cast the sound to the ends of the room. Posture and purpose.

This all feels like excellent advice for life and for creativity.

But, as I reminded my sister, it was with upright posture and forward momentum in pursuit of the great purpose of watering an outdoor plant that had faded in the heat that I rammed my little toe into the leg of a chair, causing pain and limping for weeks. So there must be some caveats to all this good advice that I have not yet learned about.

I need to at least make sure I'm maintaining a posture and positiveness that will allow ideas and creativity to come, not curl up into concerns and idle distractions, eyes on the ground. I can feel bad about not writing, but need to remember that there's not-doing and there's being. It occurs to me that this notion of posture and purpose can at least pull me from a slouch of not-doing to a stance of being. But it seems like I shouldn't make any sudden movements. Or at least wear shoes.

*

Go outside. Walk if you can, run maybe, or sit and look around. Breathe. Deliberately do NOT write for three days. Relax. Renew. Start again.

PART TWO:

The Revision Process

I. Beneath the Skin: or, Levels of Editing Poems, An Overview

What is a poem? A made thing—poured onto the page, nudged onto the page, spat onto the page…and then worked: carved, smoothed, questioned, made exact. I'm not sure anything that does not undergo that process should be called a poem, but rather some other word: a thing, a whatsit, a lump of something that might be something.

Revision can be thought of as choice-making. Although choices are made along the way as we create, it's in review and consideration that we can linger to make choices informed by intention. But they have to be led by the made thing, not our hopes and dreams for the made thing.

It seems to me that revision can be focused on three levels:

> ☞ the text on the page
> > ☞ intention
> > > ☞ what I think of as ambition

It is hard to revise one's own work. But it is necessary to grow the tough skin and fierce attention to do so, or to allow someone else to wade in and do it along with you. It is the only way to create good work.

Mind you, I'm rarely focused and together enough to work at all these levels with any given poem, and am largely lazy anyway. But it occurs to me that this is the bar I'd like to set for myself in the editing process. And by "bar," I mean, let me belly up to it and order a whiskey for the ordeal.

Try out my basic arsenal of editing approaches:

- ☞ Walk away from the fresh poems for a couple of weeks.
- ☞ Plot the logic of your arguments/analogies to make sure they are solid.
- ☞ Take out entire sections that seem to wander off track.
- ☞ Break them apart and put them back together differently.
- ☞ Rewrite them backwards to try to get some insights or surprises.
- ☞ Ask a trusted poet friend to take a look at them and try the edits they suggest, even if every part of you is saying *no no no*. You never know what you might learn from the exercise.
- ☞ Try combining two related poems into one.
- ☞ Do a writing exercise starting with the thought: *What I'm really trying to say is…*

II. Do Be Do Be Do; or, the Power and Necessity of Active Verbs

I was listening to someone read a short fiction piece recently and was struck at the leap in power when she came to a character's gesture. For all the loveliness of the prose telling who, why, and where, it was the act of the characters—he reached toward her throat, she grabbed after the falling ring—that caught and carried the energy of the piece. Someone else read a poem and again, it was not the abstract nouns, for all their romantic evocations, that contained the poem's weight, but the verb that snapped out and struck.

I just read Robert MacFarlane's *Landmarks*, a wonderful book about books and words, specifically words of regional dialect that describe things specific to regional experiences: how the fog creeps across the moor, the way certain rock formations sparkle, how the regular passage of a small animal through a hedge creates a hole. Worlds and worlds, words and worlds.

I think of Rilke in "Ninth Elegy": Maybe we are here to say: house, bridge, fountain, gate, pitcher, fruit, tree, window…. (Well, is the best translation "pitcher"? Or is is it "jug"? "Carafe"?) Looking through my recent drafts I think I've gone slack with language.

Good writing demands strong verbs, motion, gestures. Power lurks in the acts of the hands, the body, the feet, trunk or petal, wing or Mack truck. Don't give me love. Give me the actions that love compels.

Examine all the verbs in your draft, and act to wake up those verbs, make them carry more weight, move with more fleetness.

III. Line Item; or, On Poetic Lineation

A line should start strong and end strong as much as possible, and should have some reason for being a made line that ends deliberately and with purpose rather than one that ends because you think a line should be about so long, or one that haphazardly strolls across the page until the automatic right margin shunts it downward.

A line must have some integrity. That integrity should be in the form of:

- **idea**—that is, it should do the work of building on, refuting, suggesting something other than, developing or moving along the idea of the poem

- **rhythm**—the line should have some relationship to the lines around it such that it carries along or disrupts established rhythms

- **sound**—the sounds in the line should have some kind of resonance with the idea of the poem or, again, be part of a larger sonic pattern in the poem

The line break itself should have a purpose—to suggest, to control the reader's pace: hurry the reader along or stop them in their tracks, to hint or wink, to emphasize, argue, and again it also can have sonic responsibilities in the form of, well, silence.

Not every line in every poem necessarily carries weight. Sometimes you just have to get from point A to point B. But the editing process should include serious consideration of each line and its integrity. This is the great fun of writing poetry, for heaven's sake! Otherwise, just write prose. Prose is fine too.

Try three different approaches to the line in one of your poems-in-progress: chop them short, throw them around the page, let them scroll. What did you learn? What serves the poem best?

Check the first word of each line in your poem. Are they small and dull: e.g., "it," "to," "the"? Can some of those lines begin more interestingly?

IV. On the Sentence

Award-winning Canadian author Doug Glover has a book of essays on writing called, characteristic of his humor, *The Erotics of Restraint: Essays on Literary Form*. Poems too consist of sentences, and his wisdom is every bit as useful for writers of poetry. Here in an adapted extraction published on TheWalrus.ca, Glover speaks volumes about sentences:

☞ "One day, I happened to read an essay called 'On Some Technical Elements of Style in Literature' by Robert Louis Stevenson. He was talking about sentences, but instead of repeating platitudes, he showed how to construct sentences on the basis of conflict. Instead of just announcing a single thesis, a sentence begins by setting out two or more contrasting ideas; the sentence develops a conflict, intensifying toward a climax, a 'knot' Stevenson calls it, and then, after a moment of suspension, slides easily toward a close."

☞ "Suddenly writing a sentence became an exciting prospect, a journey of discovery, a miniature story with a conflict and a plot, the outcome of which I might not know at the outset."

☞ "The lesson is to inject conflict, rhythm, plot, and energy into your sentences by deploying relatively simple forms. Never leave a crude sentence snoozing on the page when there is the possibility of dramatic elaboration."

And so inspired, I to the sentence fall back again, retreat—retreat!—to the beginning—or, is it really the beginning, or some waypoint on the spiral?—to begin again, to roll/push/shove/muscle/spin/turn/revolve/cycle/trundle my rock of carbuncled words and sentences up the rubbled hillside.

Write a long one-sentence poem.

Write a short poem in which each line is a complete sentence.

Intersperse one poem with the other. Get crazy. What did you learn?

V. Word Choice = Tone

As I brood upon my problematic new poems I think most of them suffer from, at the very least, a problem of tone. They sound overly grandiose, like I've suddenly taken on a British accent or something. I want to say to the poem, "Get over yourself."

The poems are stumbling around some fairly abstract concepts and this tone is the trap I often fall into when I'm writing from an intellectual interest in an idea rather than from a more visceral reaction to some stimulus. But I love poems that do a good job of getting their fingers gripped onto the elbow of a good hardy abstract concept. I know it can be done.

There is one recent poem of mine whose tone I love but the poem itself goes nowhere. I think the problem with that poem is it doesn't have a central concept around which it's stumbling. The balance of idea and tone is crucial; one must match the other, and one cannot move forward without the other, it seems.

It occurs to me that one of the revision approaches I can take with tone is to radically pare down the words, to move away and away from prose, to introduce white space and silence. Sometimes this can unsettle the plummy tone and begin to allow the poem to get its feet under it.

In contrast, with the poem that goes nowhere, one approach I can take is to keep writing, to write toward something, often starting with the prompt "what I'm really trying to say is:". Then once I've got a lot of prosaic words that are heading me toward the central idea the poem is wanting to consider, I can begin paring back toward something interesting.

Take one of your poems-in-progress and rewrite it as a gossipy letter to a friend.

Rewrite it as a scientific article.

Rewrite it as an instruction manual.

In doing so, did you discover any useful words to plug into the orginal? A new and useful angle or point of view?

VI. Syntax; or, I saw a bear driving down the road this morning

I've been thinking about syntax, a word derived from the Greek "together + arrange," itself an interesting syntax. So much power in the order of things. The images on a totem pole not only themselves have meaning, but their order on the pole and their juxtaposition with other images also has meaning, so a totem pole has syntax. And syntax is not just a linear project, but something more like an electron cloud, or the appendage-y human body, "the hip bone connected," as it were.

E. E. Cummings was a master at subverting the expected order of words in a sentence, torquing the linear thought, surprising us, sometimes confusing us, but often showing us the world in a new way, crimping and jumbling the Venetian blinds of our view. His work suggests to me that order is mutable, and interesting things come when the rules of order are questioned, are loosened.

Not only do I find the exercise of playing with the syntax of the sentences of my poem a useful editing activity, but I suspect there's something to be learned here about life too. Every time I hit a birthday I wonder if I shouldn't be doing such-and-such at this stage in my life, or shouldn't I have accomplished *x* or *y* by now. But if I think of my life as a syntax unique to my nature and circumstance, then I can give myself a break. I can embrace the "somewhere i have never travelled," can imagine glimpsing a bear driving an Impala through the quiet morning.

Rewrite each sentence (and/or each line) backwards, from the bottom up.
Discover anything fun?

VII. The Visual

How does the poem want to look on the page? Is it stoutly clinging to the left margin? Does it splay itself across the space? Does it call for the march of couplets, or long to be one solid chunk of text? Does it flower in the form of a traditional sonnet? Does it present itself best in a long tail of two-beat lines? I consider such questions consciously, ruled not by my willful mind, but by the demands of the poem.

It drives me insane when the non-poet world casually sets a poem center-justified on the page, as if Hallmark has adjudicated and decided the course of all poems. I've even seen a respected print journal do this to every single poem that it features on a webpage each month. I will never submit my work to that journal.

All my poems start left-justified. But I've had some of them almost physically reach out and kick me, so insistent are they to have some white space breathed in to them. I've also spread poems out onto the page that tangle themselves up and need to be reset with less chaos and more order. I try stanza breaks both orderly and disorderly to discover what might be suggested by the breaks.

Recently I've been experimenting in my poetry with placing far more white on the page among words than I have ever done before. We had an interesting conversation about this at my recent writing retreat—how do you decide where the space goes in such a setting?

Natural pauses, deliberate choices to withhold information or make the reader wait, and some instinct about what words or phrases could use the kind of emphasis that silence around them can provide was our best approximation for an equation for such decisionmaking.

Sometimes I fear it makes the poem look too self-conscious on the page. Ooh, look at me all spread out here. But mostly I like it. It eases me somehow to allow some light and space into these poems I've been working on, and even imposing them on old poems in revision. Nothing worse than a poem that barks at you from the page, incessant, tied to a pole in the backyard.

*

Take a compact poem and ease it out across the page.
Play with where you put the white space.

Take a space-y poem and pull it back to the margin.

What changes? Any surprises?

VIII. And Now to Review

Here are some questions to help investigate the text on the page each time you return to a poem:

- Are the verbs active and surprising enough?

- Are the nouns specific and image-based enough?

- Are there too many articles? Not enough?

- Are the adjectives and adverbs necessary and are they doing enough heavy lifting?

- Are the line breaks serving purposes?

- Do most of the lines have integrity or heft (rather than just being throwaway lines to get to the next meaty bit)?

- Is punctuation serving clarity? If you've eschewed punctuation, is that serving the poem?

- Have you paid attention to sound and silence and rhythm? Are they serving the poem?

- If you're using a form, does the content serve the form or the form serve the content?

- Could the use of more white space serve the poem?

IX. The Bigger Picture: Intention

To focus on the intention of the poem is to pull back far enough to see both the poem on the page and yourself in the chair. You can ask of yourself and of the poem some probing questions:

- ☞ Now that you've spilled out your poem, what have you discovered about it?

- ☞ Is the poem doing what you intended, expressing what you want to express? (Do you know what you are trying to express?)

- ☞ Is it trying too hard? Is it not trying hard enough?

- ☞ Have you brought enough emotional/philosophical depth to the undertaking?

- ☞ Are the images/experiences/ideas sufficiently and deeply, specifically personal such that they become universal?

I have to consider whether I have done justice to the originating impulse, whether I have effectively shown what is at stake in these thoughts, situations, these descriptions, flights of fancy. I have to truly plumb what these poems are "about" for me.

Some people talk about considering "what is at stake" in the work. What is ever at stake in a mere poem? No lives are lost or saved here. But we are an uttering animal. We cry out in words. We jubilate in words. A poem can be a little cannon of power. What's at stake? If the reader doesn't feel that something vital is at hand, some deep energy impelled the poem to being, then the poem misses the mark. I can indulge in memory and fantasy and philosophical meanderings. I can tell you my dream. But if I have not conveyed the deep "why" of what turned those into utterance, then I am wasting the reader's time.

Take a poem you feel is not going somewhere yet. Try ending it with "I am telling you this because..." and let the next words fall where they may. Possibly keep repeating the phrase and completing it differently each time.

Should any of these lines become part of the poem, or do any of them help you understand where the poem needs to change, to grow?

X. The Bigger Picture: Doubt

I'm in this place of doubt—not necessarily doubt about my work, but doubt about my ability to understand what in the work is working. And what isn't. I know I've been here before. I know the mood has passed. I don't know if I had discovered some way out of this fog, or whether it's just time, and distraction. I've forgotten.

I've gotten a couple of acceptances just recently that I'm very pleased about. And it has also thus far been a year of many rejections. I have certain pieces I've really believed in that just keep getting rejected over and over again, and I'm losing my confidence. Do I really know how to assess my own work? Am I just wrong? My rational self says, "Yes, sometimes you're wrong. But sometimes," it assures, "you're not wrong. It's just that this is the game—send stuff out, get it rejected, repeat."

But, I argue, how do I know when I'm right and when I'm wrong?

Rational Self says, "Oh, um…is that the phone? I think I hear the phone. Gotta go…"

I come back to two things: that time is the best editor; and that there is something at gut-level that knows things about my work. But when time and gut still say it likes a work that has been getting rejected for years? I've written about honing one's own editorial sense. But can I really believe myself?

I dunno.

Rational Self rolls her eyes.

The editing process takes inner calm, perspective, and confidence. This is especially true when it comes to "knowing" that something is ready to send out. Too often I send stuff out too soon, get it back rejected, and suddenly see a new editing angle. But hey, it's a process.

But there are some times in which I just can't muster up the guts to do good editing on my own work, or see it with a sufficiently cold eye. (And I do think there are some of my works that I'll just never get perspective on. I'm just going to love their flawed selves and that's it. I'll tuck them into a manuscript somehow or incorporate them into a visual project maybe. But I won't abandon them to my C-level folder! I won't!)

A friend of mine who breeds and raises dogs talks about puppy panic periods: something a puppy did without fear a day before suddenly turns into a whites-around-the-eyes, stiff-legged-no-way-I-ain't-doin'-that trembling mess, and soon pretty much everything freaks it out. The periods generally only last a few days, although the puppy might have another such period some time later in its development.

I think I have puppy panic periods throughout my whole life. Different things set me off at different times (there are some things, of course, that set me off EVERY time). (Spider!) I think I must be in one now. Time will move me off the dime, and I'll regain my self-confidence, and/or regain some perspective on those pieces that have received consistent rejections, and/or continue to believe in them beyond all reason. Right now, though, I'm going to just sit here quietly for a while.

Take a poem that you feel doubtful of. Add to that poem a series of questions that, at least for a short time, will be part of the poem. Let the poem itself do the doubting, and see what can be learned from its questions.

XI. Know When to Run; or, When Work in Progress Is Not Making Progress; or, Giving Up As Part of Revision

I have been stuck on a couple of poems. They didn't do what I wanted them to do, resisted even doing something different, resisted any effectiveness in coming together in a way that made me satisfied. I think I pulled out my entire arsenal of editing ideas.

Nothing worked. And so it goes. So I add them to my pages and pages of abandoned poems.

It's sad to abandon an effort. I keep the pages of abandoned poems around and revisit them occasionally, hoping some new insight will enable me to save them. I cannot recall a single instance of this working.

Part of working toward being a good writer is knowing when to walk away. Part of working toward being a good writer is asking enough of your poems that some of them just can't make the bar. Sometimes whatever the impulse was to speak just does not lead to something worth hearing.

✻

For a poem you cannot revive, write a farewell to its departing self.

XII. Trust

A friend and I were looking at poem and her rewrite of it. She was trying to decide which, in the end, was the better version. I noticed in the first poem she had a plethora of images, but they did not seem to come out of each other or otherwise necessarily work together. In her rewrite, she, rightly, got rid of some of the images, but then she replaced them with abstract words. And it occurred to me that her rewrite was informed by mistrust. She doubted her poem. And so when she reached for ways to revise it, she leaped toward the next version with doubt instead of with trust. And she didn't stick the landing.

So somehow the editing process has to start with trust in the original impulse for the poem, so that the leap for the next version comes not from an unbalanced stance but from a—oh, I don't know, I can't stretch the gymnast conceit that far, as I never was even able to do a backbend and my somersaults ended up like Harriet the Spy practicing to be an onion. But you get my meaning—I need to start the editing process from a belief in the poem.

If I start the revision process with a sense of "Let's say this poem was born of a strong impulse and I can trust that enough to move forward," I might be able to move toward a revision that affirms that faith in the poem. And thusly girded, I can somersault onward, a pearl onion heading for gravy.

Take a poem that you know you need to revise. Copy it over, making little changes as they occur to you, if they occur to you, and every few lines, insert, "I believe in your..." or "I believe in these..." and complete that sentence as an address to the poem. Use this anaphora to dig into the poem itself with your conviction that this poem is worth the effort.

XIII. Ambition

And it's always useful to pause in the entire enterprise now and then to ask, "Why am I doing this? Why is my attention on this?" Even if you're unable to answer, the question is worth asking in order to refocus, to re-center.

We're all writing in or responding to a literary history and tradition. We workers in the field of the word shouldn't be afraid to consider ourselves as part of that tradition. Where do your poems fit in that tradition? Who among your literary forebears are you in coversation with?

When you are examining each poem, why not ask where your poem fits in that tradition, what poems are the greatest expression of that tradition, and does your poem reach for that greatness?

In other words, have you figured out the magic of the poems you most admire and have you sought in your own poem to create that magic?

✱

Okay, pull out all the poems. You know what to do.

PART THREE:

Submitting Your Work

You Know You Want To

Ugh. I know. But what is a writer without a reader? What is a poem without a mind for it to enter and move around inside? Don't hide your poems under a bushel. Let 'em shine shine shine. Or at least take the bushel off 'em by participating in the submission process.

Here's what everyone should know about submission: It's a numbers game.

The more places you send to and the wider your net, the more chance you have to get a yes or two. Experts in probability and statistics might argue the point, but it's been my experience. I need to send to at least twenty places to eke out a yes, usually. Ugh. I know.

☞ How to find the places you should send to?

Read read read. Subscribe to some literary magazines, pick up some at a bookstore, see if your library offers any. Take a look at the annual *Best American Poetry* anthology and see what you like and where it was first published. Find some poets whose work is like yours and research where they've published. Join some poetry groups on social media and find out what lit mags they're talking about. Take a look at your local and regional newspapers and magazines and see if they publish poetry. (If they don't, call them up and propose a monthly poetry column, or a special poetry section during April, which is national "Poetry Month," and then solicit work from local and regional poets, thereby getting to know some of your clan.)

"Yeah, but," you say, "isn't it all about who you know?" Or, "Yeah, but I don't have a publishing record or an MFA so what am I going to say in my bio?" Or, "Yeah, but I don't have time!" Maybe in some top notch magazines, it is about who you know. Those are not your magazines. Yet.

☞ What about that bio?

No one cares what's in your bio. And, no, no one cares what your cat's name is or that your children are beautiful. If you have nothing to say in your bio just give your general location in the world. "Joey Schmoey writes from her kitchen overlooking a dumpster just off 29th Street in Newark." That's fine. That's actually pretty interesting.

☞ ## Bu..bu..but, I don't have TIME!

And time? Yes, it can be time consuming. But give it ten minutes a day, or ten minutes a week, or one hour a month. Just give it a little chunk of time. A chunk here a chunk there, pretty soon you have a submission practice.

☞ ## How do I keep track of it all?

Make sure you have some way to keep track of your submissions. There are programs that help you do this, like Duotrope, about which I know nothing. There are spreadsheets and Googley doc-y things and whatnot, about which I know nothing. I have a Word document with a shit-ton of lit mags, their web pages, some info about what they're looking for and when and if there's a fee. I list each poem I send under the lit mag title and when I sent it, and I highlight it. When the rejection comes in, I unhighlight it and find another mag to send to. When a poem gets accepted, I highlight it in green and add it to my Poems I've Published list. That's just me.

☞ ## Rejections?!?!?

You will get rejections. Lots of them. Most of your submissions will be rejected. It's the cold truth.

A "no" does not mean your poem sucked. It MIGHT mean your poem sucked. But it does not DEFINITELY mean your poem sucked. Take a look at a rejected poem. Do you still like it? Send it back out.

A "yes" from a magazine once does not mean you will EVER IN THE REST OF YOUR MISERABLE LIFE GET ACCEPTED BY THAT MAGAZINE AGAIN. Trust me on this. But sometimes it does. Sometimes your work has tickled the fancy of an editor, and you've gained a fan. This is no small thing.

☞ So much money!!!

Should you pay for submissions to literary magazines? There's a whole lot of discussion around this, none of which I'm interested in reproducing here. It's entirely up to you. I don't. But I'm a cheap son of a bitch. I try to support the poetry world by buying people's books, and buying magazines, subscribing to different magazines, or submitting to contests that offer a subscription as part of the entry. I "give back" to the poetry world by offering proofreading services for free to a couple of publishers and/or act as a first-round reader for their submissions. I encourage people when I can, pass the word around on upcoming calls for submissions or good publishers or magazines I've worked with, or I offer workshops now and then or this: sharing my own experiences. That's how I support poetry. Not through paying lit mag submission fees. But see above regarding "cheap." See above regarding "it's up to you."

It's a numbers game, and indeed I do think of it (I mean, when I'm not lying prostrate, having thrown myself to the floor declaring "I'm quitting writing forever" or exclaiming "Everyone clearly hates my work, nay, hates ME") as a game, as play—both the writing and the submission. Because when you play, you laugh. And if you can't laugh, well, you might as well take your ball and go home. And what's the fun in that?

☞ Ugh, this sucks

Speaking of "fun," the submission process does not have to be done alone in a dungeon. It could be a party! Invite some poetry friends who are in the same ready-dread-y state with regard to submissions. Spend a couple of hours doing it in good company.

I have belonged for 20 years to a group we call the Women of Mass Dispersion (WMDs). Although the group has shifted focus over time, we began meeting monthly to support each other in the dreary task of submitting, getting rejected, falling on the floor moaning, quitting, starting again. We kept each other on task for finishing projects we'd begun, sending out what we'd finished, revising, rethinking, resending. Et-freaking-cetera. For a while, we'd celebrate each rejection with champagne…until that became…er…unwise… Now, something like 16 books, countless lit mag acceptances, an MFA earned, and a memorable group reading at an Irish bar later, we're still at it, a little less frequently, a little more slowly, with a tad less regularity, but still at it.

☞ Is all this worth it?

I have on a shelf a growing bulk of lit mags that have my work in them as well as a growing green-lit list of Poems I've Published in print and online. I have two books and two chapbooks of my work on those shelves, plus some books I collaborated with other poets on, plus a couple of anthologies my work is in. (I've been at this a long time.) Plus I've made videopoems, I've collaborated with a choreographer to bring some poems to the dance stage, I'm working with a musician and a visual artist on a project. It's been a grand run of playing with words, and I will play on.

I hope you will too.

PART FOUR:

Putting Together a Manuscript:

Everything I Can Think Of

I. The Collective

You have been working diligently. You discover one day that you have 50 or 60 poems, maybe more, and you think, gee, it's high time I had a book of poetry published. Turns out that putting together a manuscript is another form of revision.

What comes first? I'm not talking chicken/egg, I'm talking about which of the poems in the pile in front of you should come first? Gaah! you cry. This will not be the last time you cry gaah, but here are some ways to approach the process.

You are putting together a collection of poems, so you might take a moment and think about the collective. A bunch of disparate poems may not a collection maketh. Nor does a tight group of thematically or otherwise related poems necessarily make a good collection. Too much difference makes a collection feel random. Too much sameness makes a collection feel boring.

If you've been lucky in your life, at some point you've been a member of a group that has cohered, has been able to embrace a level of diversity, strengthen the connective tissues, and make of itself a functioning thing. Experiences like this are fun, and fine. This is what you want to make of your poems. I was part of a singing group that started as the Five Fabulous Females. Tall, short, prim, ribald, soprano, contralto, Broadway-oriented, bluesy. Viva les différences. Things quickly fell apart, however, as one member seemed to want different things from the group through a different process, and we never actually performed together as five. Then we were Four Fabulous Females. A performance or two later, things fell apart as one member seemed to approach things with a different sensibility to the rest. Then there were three. We three went on to perform together many times and remain friends to this day. So it goes. You could put out a collection of poems some of which live uneasily with each other. Or you could hold out for a good team.

So, taking a deep breath, ruthlessly read through the poems, and by instinct and without much thought, put to one side poems that cause a little hitch in your confidence, a tiny question of readiness, any momentary hesitation. They might be able to be saved, but for this first round, anything questionable has to be put aside. Don't worry about how many you've set aside and how many are left. You want the core of your manuscript to be the best poems you have. Then anything new you have to generate or revise, you know you need to raise to the same standard.

II. Ordering the Disorderly

There are all kinds of ways to order poems. Try as many as you can think of, but keep in mind the idea of "collective." I attended a dance performance recently in which one piece was made up of short dances to 24 short pieces of music. In the end, I felt that what we'd watched was 24 short dances, not one coherent dance. The performance seemed to go on and on because there was no arc connecting the dances together. The same can be found in poetry collections. Try to find and highlight some kind of connective tissue, to reveal some kind of arc.

Go through again the group that is left and again in a quick sort, without too much thought, mark poems that seem to be addressing similar themes or issues. Maybe put a different color dot for different themes.

Your chosen poems may be falling into natural groupings. Should you make them into discrete sections? Not all manuscripts have to have sections. But sections can help to focus the collective attention of both the poems and the reader. So if groups seem to fall naturally into sections, make sections. If not, don't worry about it.

You will likely have some outliers. It could be that they belong to another manuscript altogether. You will feel panicked by this, because you have now lost a number of poems and no longer have a full length collection. This is the way things go. Better to build from a good base than to shove 60 random poems together and hope they work.

You will probably come to find that there are poems that seem to want to be in close proximity and poems that do not. You should begin to find that some kinds of bunches work together and some do not. You may begin to feel that too much similarity of some of the poems will dictate that they should be spread throughout the manuscript, their similarity functioning as stitches that tie the whole thing together. Trust this process.

Go through the group again that is left from the Part I process and...

- ☞ Mark in some other way poems that are similar in form or approach.

- ☞ Mark in some other way poems that use similar imagery perhaps or share some other similarity.

- ☞ Now put all the like-themed poems together. You might find several streams of themes—put the groups in some (at this point perhaps random) order and read through the whole thing. Make any notes on what you've learned or poems that seemed particularly well suited together and poems that were too similar and should not appear next to each other.

☞ Now maybe reorder them using the form markers and read through again. Make your notes.

☞ Now reorder in whatever other similarity markers you have used and read through the whole thing again. Make your notes.

☞ This is exhausting and you will periodically want to just go to the top of the stairs and throw them down and then leave them in whatever order is left when you clean them up. This is also legitimate. Do it. Read through and make notes.

III. Filling It In

At one point I thought I had a manuscript just because I had a bunch of poems I wrote in a certain (lengthy!) period of time. But in the end it felt like a collected works instead of a slice of a concentrated period of a mind working. In the end, as a collection it did itself a disservice by meandering and feeling jumbled and uneven after a while. I had to identify some central concerns and…yes…write new poems. Once you have a pile of your best work set in some kind of order, you will begin to see where the gaps are and/or where you need to create more work that supports and lengthens what you've collected thus far. Thus your assignment: write on.

Once you've put together a themed group of poems, look for the holes. Write the poem that fills one of those empty spaces.

IV. But Wait

Give some thought to what the collection is getting at, what themes are being considered, what of your obsessions are being visited, or are you exploring a kind of form, or an image, or a period of time, a person, an event. Make notes about ideas that began to be addressed in the collection but petered out, about forms or images that began to be addressed in the collection but petered out, about forms or images that now seem to stick out like the collection has bed head. Note if there are too many mentions of one thing (a friend noticed in one of my collections that I seem to have an obsession with teeth), and note satisfying threads and echoing imagery.

If you had to write a blurb for the back of your book, what would it say? Once you've captured that, are there poems that clearly lie too far outside that statement? Maybe put them aside for another collection.

V. Take a Step Farther Back

You will not thank me for this, but I have to raise the issue: Is what you're saying compelling? Is how you're saying it compelling? The fact is the poetry publishing world is competitive. Many able poets are writing very competent poems in collections that are not very interesting. Many interesting writers are offering collections that are not very competently written. Why not strive to be both writing well and thinking deeply, imaginatively. Push your work into places where you don't entirely know your way. Wonder does wonders for work. Imaginative + vivid + fully felt = winning combination. By imaginative, I mean evidence of a lively mind at work. By vivid, I mean something special in the language (my preference) or the form or the approach. By fully felt, I mean some emotional heft.

I was reading a manuscript of someone else's poems recently, and they were really good poems. Very competent, lovely poems of domesticity and parenthood. But, I thought to myself, some element is missing. Is the problem that I'm just not that interested in poems of domesticity and parenthood? I didn't think that was it. I decided finally that what I was missing was a kind of reaching. This very able poet was not reaching beyond her grasp. She knew the world of her poems too well. If I call what I wanted from this manuscript more risk-taking, what do I mean by that? It's a sense, I think, of a mind in motion rather than a mind at rest; questions asked and pondered rather than answered. What does it mean for any of us to take risks in our work? How do I write a poem that feels risky to me, that feels like I'm peering over the edge of something, and something that makes the reader tremble there too? Is risk about subject area, form, language, meaning?

A friend says, "I demand emotional risk. Not necessarily confessional, but someone willing to open a vein, or why are we there anyway?" I think I agree about "emotional risk," but I'm just not always sure what that means—both in what I read and in what I write. And I actually don't always need "emotional" risk, but SOME kind of reaching, whether emotional, craftish, wordish, conceptual.

You do not want to hear this. You do not want to do this. You may not have sufficient distance to look at the collection from this perspective yet. Either put the collection away for a little while until you can get a fresh perspective, or…ignore me and sally forth. Whatever you do, do not give up.

*

Where has this set of poems been afraid to go? Have they been circling but not getting to the center? Write the poem that "goes too far," that goes into that fearful space.

VI. Where To Begin

There is likely one poem you think is terrific and should open the collection, and one or two poems that feel conclusionary in some way. You may be wrong. Don't settle too quickly on the opening poem. It may very well be the last decision to be made, once you settle in to the feel of the whole manuscript.

The first poem should teach the reader how to read the whole manuscript. It should give some sense of what the reader can expect.

The last poem should open out somehow, so the reader feels like they've opened a new door back into their own life through which they see things differently.

This is a lot to ask of opening and closing poems, I know. But if our reach does not attempt to succeed our grasp, etcetera.

Make a list of 5-7 different poems from your collection that could possibly be "the starter poem." Let each candidate audition for the spot for a couple of days, just to see what they've got.

Then do the same for your "finale" poem. Let your mind be changed a few times.

VII. And Then

Proofread. Proofread. Proofread.

Regarding typeface and format: Make sure the way you designate titles is simple—all caps for example, or bold. Don't make it too fancy. But make it consistent. The same goes for section headings. In headings and text, don't use obscure tyepfaces. If you are playing with spacing or other odd presentation on the page, be prepared to submit your work as a .pdf in case transmittal screws up your careful play.

VIII. The End

Make sure every poem kicks ass. The more poems you put into a collection, the more likely it is that you'll include ones that aren't as strong as others, which weakens the collection. Remember, there are a lot of poets out there, and a lot of people doing really good work. Be one of them.

Books and Articles I Mention, and One I Didn't Mention But Want To Make Note of Because It's Practically an MFA-in-a-Book:

Lynda Barry, *Syllabus: Notes from an Accidental Professor*, Drawn and Quarterly, 2014.

Stephen Dobyns, *Best Words, Best Order: Essays on Poetry*, Palgrave Macmillan, 1996, 2nd ed. 2003.

Northrop Frye, "The Archetypes of Literature," *Kenyon Review*, Winter 1951, accessed online 2025, https://kenyonreview.org/kr-online-issue/kenyon-review-credos/selections/northrop-frye-656342/.

Douglas Glover, *The Erotics of Restraint: Essays on Literary Form*, Biblioasis, 2019; excerpt "The Power of a Good Sentence," *The Walrus*, accessed 2025: https://thewalrus.ca/the-power-of-a-good-sentence/.

Vivian Gornick, *The Situation and the Story: The Art of Personal Narrative*, Farrar, Straus & Giroux, 2002.

Brenda Hillman, "Cracks in the Oracle Bone," Poetry Foundation, 2010, accessed 2025: https://www.poetryfoundation.org/articles/69568/cracks-in-the-oracle-bone-teaching-certain-contemporary-poems.

John McPhee, *Draft No. 4: Notes on the Writing Process*, Farrar, Straus & Giroux, 2018.

Richard Russo, *The Destiny Thief: Essays on Writing, Writers and Life*, Knopf, 2018.

About the Author

Marilyn McCabe's work has won contests and awards, including: Grayson Books chapbook contest, resulting in publication of *Being Many Seeds*; A Room of Her Own Foundation's Orlando Prize; the Word Works Hilary Tham Capital Collection call resulting in publication of *Perpetual Motion*; and two artist grants from the New York State Council on the Arts. Other published collections are *Glass Factory* and *Rugged Means of Grace*. Her videopoetry has appeared in international film festivals, including a win in the experimental film category at the Albany Film Festival, in art galleries, on public television, and online. She blogs about writing and reading at Owrite:MarilynOnaRoll..wordpress.com and on the podcast "Whirled Through a Poem's Eye."

About the Artist

Jennifer Sattler is an award-winning children's book author/illustrator and painter. This embroidered work on linen is part of a triptych. She lives and works in upstate New York and Vermont.

About The Word Works

Since its founding in 1974, The Word Works has steadily published volumes of contemporary poetry and presented public programs. Its imprints include The Washington Prize, The Tenth Gate Prize, The Hilary Tham Capital Collection, and International Editions.

Monthly, The Word Works offers free programs in its Café Muse Literary Salon. Starting in 2023, the winners of the Jacklyn Potter Young Poets Competition will be presented in the June Café Muse program.

As a 501(c)3 organization, The Word Works has received awards from the National Endowment for the Arts, the National Endowment for the Humanities, the D.C. Commission on the Arts & Humanities, the Witter Bynner Foundation, Poets & Writers, The Writer's Center, Bell Atlantic, the David G. Taft Foundation, and others, including many generous private patrons.

An archive of artistic and administrative materials in the Washington Writing Archive is housed in the George Washington University Gelman Library. The Word Works is a member of the Community of Literary Magazines and Presses.

wordworksbooks.org